Jimbo Gets his Skates on

ISBN 0 361 07155 8

Licensed by BBC Enterprises Limited
Published 1986 by Purnell Books
a division of Macdonald and Co. (Publishers) Limited
Maxwell House 74 Worship Street London EC2A 2EN
a BPCC plc company
Made and printed in Belgium

Winter had arrived at London airport and many hands were needed to keep the runways open . . .

The chief controller was hard at work

organising everybody to give a hand at clearing the snow from Runway Four.

"Follow Sammy Snow-Plough," he roared through his loudspeaker. "And don't forget your snow shovels."

"And I want Phil the Fuel Truck to put his snow chains on. It's very slippery and I don't want him getting stuck in the snow," screamed the Chief through his loudspeaker.

Amanda Baggage got told off for not having her covers on to keep the luggage dry. Tommy Tow-Truck tried to tell the Chief that she couldn't find the covers—but the Chief said it was no excuse because all she had to do was get a new one from the store.

Meanwhile, Jimbo sat out on the runway.

"Are you awake out there?" shouted the Chief over the tannoy system. "Jimbo, do you hear me?"

"Fat chance I've got of sleeping in this weather," replied Jimbo angrily. "It's freezing out here."

"I'll soon get you warmed up," said the Chief, with a wry smile. "Get your engines started and stand by for take off—now!"

"Take off?" said Jimbo, looking up at the snow. "I was looking forward to a hot water bottle in my hangar."

"Hot water is exactly what you'll be in if you don't get airborne," yelled the Chief, his face turning quite purple. "Get going!"

"Good thing I put on a woolly vest this morning," sighed Jimbo, as he coasted down the slippery runway gradually lifting his feet off the ground as he climbed skywards. "Brrr, it's cold," he shivered.

Inside the control room the Chief was busily throwing switches, until he noticed a stewardess knocking on his door. "Excuse me, Chief," she said, "but are we clear for flying today in this terrible weather? I have our wonderful ice skating team anxious to get

to Germany for the World Championships."

"Why certainly, my dear," said the Chief, switching on his microphone. "I have just the plane ready and waiting for such a situation—Jimbo, come on in—I've got an urgent job for you."

As Jimbo glided back to touch down on Runway Four, he was so busy moaning to himself about the weather that he'd forgotten about the icy runway.

As he touched the ground he immediately went into a frantic spin on the ice—slipping and sliding all the way down the runway. Tommy Tow-Truck, standing by to tow him to the passenger bay, shouted in a very loud voice.

"Steady on, Jimbo. Take it easy on this ice."

"You're right," said Jimbo, coming to a graceful skid. "Gosh, it is slippery today."

Fortunately the Chief was looking at the pretty stewardess more than he was the runway. So he missed most of Jimbo's slippery landing.

"You'll have to do better than that when you touch down in Germany, Jimbo," he said. "Particularly with our Ice Champions on board."

"Ice Champions?" replied Jimbo, wide eyed. "Hey, Chief, that is a special job—real VIP people—Great! When do I leave?"

The Championship Ice Team loaded aboard Jimbo, all banging the snow from their feet as they mounted Sammy Steps.

"I'm going to have a headache if this weather keeps up," moaned Sammy.

Once in the air, Jimbo headed quickly up above the snow clouds and out into the sunshine.

"I'll get a little sunshine on my back before I land in Germany," he said, blinking at the sun's rays.

"Hello, Germany, permission to land please," said Jimbo, banging and bumping down through the murky clouds.

"Goot-en-tag, Jimbo my friend," replied the German air controller. "Be careful how you touch down—there is much ice down on the runway."

Jimbo's passengers all fastened their seatbelts to prepare for a bumpy landing.

"Go on, Jimbo," shouted the Ice Skating Champions. "Show them how the British can ice skate."

Jimbo approached the runway and touched down one leg, twirled three times and with a final skip and a jump slid gracefully to a halt in front of the busy German passenger air terminal.

A great cheer came up from the crowd

waiting to greet the British Ice Champions. A judge shouted for technical marks, and a row of sixes were held up on cards.

"Artistic merit," shouted the judge. And the crowd held up another six marks . . .

"Wunderbar," roared the crowd.

"Full marks!" yelled the judge. And again the crowd applauded as the British Ice Skating Champions disembarked with their ice skates slung over their shoulders.

"Cheerio, Jimbo," they shouted. "We can't help but do well after such a triumphant display of ice skating."

Jimbo once again lifted skywards into the

heavy snow-filled clouds heading back to England.

"I can't wait to tell the Chief back home," he said to himself. "He'll be so proud ."

"Permission to land, Chief," said Jimbo, trying desperately to see the ground through the thick grey clouds.

"Sorry, Jimbo," replied the Chief. "We're up to our ears in snow down here—I can't see you getting down before dawn. You'll have to divert to Manchester."

"Oh come on, Chief," said Jimbo wearily. "I'm tired, I've had a hard day, I want to cuddle up in my warm little hangar and thaw out."

"Don't be silly, Jimbo," said the Chief, sipping his cup of hot bedtime cocoa. "It'll take Sammy Snow-Plough all night to clear that runway—it's thick with drifting snow."

"Well, I'm coming in," said Jimbo angrily. "I've got no passengers aboard, so I've only got myself to look after—here I come, Chief . . ."

And before the Chief could swallow his mouthful of hot cocoa, Jimbo dropped out of the sky and grabbed two poles from the end of Runway Four as he swept in through the driving snow.

Then with the poles tucked firmly under his wings he slid in on top of the firm snow, just like a champion skier would ski down a mountainside.

"Where did you learn to do that?" shouted

the Chief over the tannoy as Jimbo coasted to a sliding halt right outside his hangar.

"It's a little trick I learned while I was over in Germany," said Jimbo, winking at Tommy Tow-Truck.

"We are the champions!" sang Tommy as he towed Jimbo into his warm little hangar for the night out of the icy cold weather.